Alan D. Butcher

THE SILENCE OF THE NORTH

The Arctic Sonnets

BookLand press

Published by BookLand Press
15 Allstate Parkway, Suite 600, Markham, Ontario L3R 5B4
www.booklandpress.com

Printed and bound in Canada.

Library and Archives Canada Cataloguing in Publication

Butcher, Alan D.
The silence of the North: Arctic sonnets / Alan D. Butcher.

ISBN 978-1-926956-15-2

1. Canada, Northern--Poetry. I. Title.

PS8603.U829S55 2012 C811'.6 C2012-901865-1

Canada Council for the Arts Conseil des arts du Canada
ONTARIO ARTS COUNCIL
CONSEIL DES ARTS DE L'ONTARIO

We acknowledge the support of the Canada Council for the Arts, which last year invested $154 million to bring the arts to Canadians throughout the country. We acknowledge the support of the Ontario Arts Council (OAC), an agency of the Government of Ontario, which last year funded 1,681 individual artists and 1,125 organizations in 216 communities across Ontario for a total of $52.8 million. We acknowledge the financial support of the Ontario Media Development Corporation for our publishing activities.

To the Cobourg Poetry Workshop

TABLE OF CONTENTS

Prelude

A Northwest Passage, years ago, was sought.
Those days what England sought, she got – the lot;
Britannia ruled all things on sea and land.
But trade routes didn't change at her command.
Ships' time at sea was ruinously expensive;
The months to China much too funds-intensive.
You battled storms around the Horn each way;
Cape Horn was there and wouldn't go away.
You'd make it if your vessels didn't sink,
But lose two ships in three? It made you think.
The Northwest Passage would, if it were found,
Save months at sea which, money-wise, was sound.
And so the bold adventurers came forth
To cast the dice and find a new way north.
And all were 16th century Errol Flynns!
Who leaped to add to their existing sins.
New seas they sought, to glorify their name –
And Britain's, too, of course – but first came Fame!
They blithely cast all hope and sense aside
And gambled, at the mercy of the tide.

Those days Elizabeth the First looked west.
To find the Northwest Passage she'd invest:
Provided three small vessels, and decreed
Her friend Sir Martin Frobisher would lead.
To fabled China then he turned his head,
But stubbed his toe on Baffin Isle instead.
In '76 to Baffin Isle he came,

And to a tiny bay he then laid claim.
That's it: Old Frobisher just named his bay,
Set sail, went back to England straightaway.
In 1577 he returned,
Resplendent in the fame he'd scarcely earned.
Though not much was accomplished. Looked around,
And recognized the same familiar ground.
Next year another trip. Why? Heaven knows.
Make sure it still was there, I would suppose.
Sir Martin Frobisher, for one small bay,
And all the bits of ice which 'round it lay,
Spent millions on supplies and ships – for what?
When he returned, a smile was all he brought.
"Returning" was the thing that he was good at,
And so got all the practice that he could at.
Each time, he sailed back home to wild acclaim.
Achievements? None. Yet always gained in fame!
Did nothing, really, yet, by gosh, was knighted,
His northern romance left still unrequited.

But now, let's close our disapproving eye
And kiss the 16th century goodbye.
Let's move ahead in time to Montréal,
Explorers' often favoured port of call.
Mine, too; yet – brave explorer that I was –
It surely goes against all Nature's laws
To send me north to Baffin's icy halls
While southern sun my name still softly calls.
So let us pause in Montréal awhile
And weigh the days that led to Baffin's isle.

Montréal

Prologue

In Montréal while working at the Daily Star,
(A paper now defunct as many are),
I first heard word of opportunities
Up north in radar site communities.
Before, I'd been a bus boy in a bar
(a job whose skills exceeded mine by far);
I then tried selling door-to-door, and failed
(I lacked the skills that <u>*that*</u> *job, too, entailed).*
And so, not wildly skilled in any trade,
I thought that at the Star I had it made.
I ended in the Star's financial room.
In tedium or tension, bust or boom,
I'd firmly hold the ticker tape's wrong end,
The end where profit never called me friend.
The times were tight. If dimes were dynamite,
I might blow up balloons. No sleep at night …
But then I learned that there were jobs galore
Up north, beyond the coast of Labrador!
For younger hearts like mine the call was real;
For me it held immediate appeal:
A six-month contract north of 63!
The polar bears, the Inuit – and me!

1 / 1

The city streets, unsatisfying, bare,
Disharmony in every concrete block;
The city nights a sea of frank despair;
The frantic pace; the emphasis on schlock.
I can't accept the city life's descent
To moral cul-de-sacs. But now I find
Adventure's winds evict my discontent,
And leave the city's windless flags maligned:
The arctic's breath will fill my northern days!
I'll let the tundra guide my southern feet!
I'll change for one brief hour my southern ways
And walk where arctic sea and Baffin meet!
I'll let the arctic take my hand: Lead on!
To that improbable first stage: Saint John!

Saint John

Prologue

My father read his Shakespeare through and through;
Retired now, he'd nothing else to do.
"Not borrower nor lender be," said he.
Not hard to do when you're as poor as me.
To Saint John, then, with little more than clothes:
A gloomy town, its sullen face morose.
Accommodations there turned out to be
Poor structures sinking in a muddy sea,
All washed by constant rain, skies leaden, grey,
And all around: The mud that shaped our day.

1 / 1

By night train to Saint John, NB, at last.
A train old Frobisher had never known.
The land snow-burdened, dark, through which
we've passed.
Saint John: First step toward the yet unknown.
And now: Despair; anticipation's flown:
No taverns nor a cocktail lounge was there.
No lubricants to set a friendly tone;
No social life: From thirst and thought forebear.
Grey skies, and rain; no ray of sun to spare.
Within the bunkhouse some play cards, or read;
We're waiting, waiting, for the trip by air.
We'll sleep, the days of boredom will recede.
Tomorrow I'll be leaving – bless the day!
Goodbye, Saint John, and northward to Goose Bay!

Goose Bay

Prologue

Is Goose Bay just the same old muddy song?
I thought it might not be, but I was wrong.
Already I am sick of being wrong.
Am I naive, ingenuous, to long
For one small sod of Canada's green grass?
A smiling sun, without this damp morass?
Is eastern Canada just one big marsh?
Whose skies are grey, and attitude so harsh?
Yet still there is amusement of a kind,
To ease the boredom, and improve(?) the mind.
There's lots to drink, "exciting" movies, too:
John Wayne and Yanks re-fighting World War II.
Not all that good, but did I have a choice?
Afar, instead, I heard adventure's voice:
Beyond the narrow sea of Labrador
Was Baffin Isle, and Frobisher, offshore!

1 / 2

Goose Bay, I must admit, was no surprise.
It seemed at first a sketch, and poorly drawn,
Of what I'd known so well in old Saint John;
Goose Bay? No way; just Saint John in disguise.
The standard mud and sand, of course, applies.
Two zones, American and ours, were there,
By muddy pools surrounded, so beware!
And over all this bleak terrain: Grey skies.
I look around, and nothing meets my eyes;
I see no signs of life besides our own.
Just mud, and sand, and restless men alone.
Though once, I think, I heard a bird's sad cries.
Our home away from home: Stark Labrador.
A passing muddy memory, no more.

2 / 2

Those days in Goose I'll never see again.
A small town may have been there, yet who knows?
Beneath a smiling sky a friendly lane?
A house or two? A tree that somehow grows?
This muddy desolation's what we chose,
But still, there's Yankee movies, lots of beer.
The Yankee zone, however, frowns on those
Who dress the way construction work holds dear:
In ragged clothes, unshaved from ear to ear,
That's me, a typical Canadian lout.
Whose future for the moment's still unclear,
But that will pass, and so will I, no doubt.
For me there'll be just memories in store;
For now there's Baffin Isle beyond the shore.

Northern Welcome

Prologue

The wise will tell you: First impressions last.
As maxim, though, its usefulness seems past.
And yet, I think, as truth it's hard to beat,
Though last impressions will, sometimes, compete.
When first impressions are of silent snow,
Of empty land, a sullen dark plateau,
Go bet the farm, man, nothing's going to change
In this environment withdrawn and strange.
My aircraft seems suspended, while below
Are icebergs, moving ponderously, slow,
Just shadows scattered there, unformed, unplanned.
A wordless welcome to this unknown land.
It always will be as it is right now,
An Arctic frown across its Arctic brow.

1 / 3

A vast unfriendly sky now runs before,
To Frobisher, well north of 63,
Where Baffin Island's rocky northern shore
Will touch the edges of the northern sea.
Beneath the fuselage, there's rock and tree
And then the unforgiving waters there:
Ungava Bay, an irritable sea,
Where I have second thoughts expressed in prayer.
Canadian I, to this grim land the heir;
And yet, a glance shows I will never be.
I own no part; the whole, so cold and bare,
Subdues and frightens stronger souls than me.
In awe I now begin to recognize
My place in this bleak land before my eyes.

2 / 3

From southern latitudes where once we laughed,
We're shivering in this antique of the air,
On hard and narrow benches fore and aft
We're flying, dying, dying to get there.
Yet now I see, in horrified despair,
The plane's door shaking, rattling in the gale,
To my eyes, gaping wide, an inch to spare,
In this propeller-driven trash can's tail.
I see below, in frightening detail,
The frozen floating burgs of Hudson Strait.
They seem to watch me in my craft so frail,
My craft, my plane, my flying orange crate.
But there they are, a silent multitude;
The northland's welcome, distant, vast, subdued.

3 / 3

Descending now, fast-flying cloud low-lying.
Beyond: the head of frozen Frobisher Bay
Along whose rocky icy verge we're flying,
In the shadows flying, of a waning day.
Half-hidden in the snow down near the bay:
A dozen smoking huts next to the shore.
The airfield's landing strip; a hangar, grey;
A shed; a dog or two beside the door.
Nocturnal stillness seems to underscore
The hopeless world's-end aspect of the site;
A light … another over there … no more;
The tundra's vastness stretching into night.
And now, with us, that arctic night descends
On this — this land, it seems, that never ends.

Tent

Prologue

Why me? Why there? An empty 12-man tent
That stressed the hostile air the tundra lent.
But why alone? I could not fathom this.
A strange hello? The north's sardonic kiss?
A joke perhaps? My workmates' levity?
For them a hearty ho-ho-ho, but me?
No laughs from me, my sense of humour fled.
Imagination touched my lonely bed;
My mind sensed cold companions in the night;
Strange visions rose, on shadowed wings took flight.
All night the visions haunted me, till dawn;
Cruel visions, on my mind's grey canvas drawn.

1 / 2

O southerner, on this your first dark night,
Alone within your tent (the 12-man size) …
Alone? I ask; the wind alone replies,
Its wordless voice I heard, its comfort slight.
Is someone … some *thing* else abroad tonight?
I knew not what it meant, or what it was,
Or yet its dark intent or darker cause.
Just that a … *presence* lay beyond my sight.
Strange circumstance: The wind's nocturnal flight,
And me, surrounded by this canvas sea.
Mais oui! A dozen empty 12-man tents — and me!
Yet … was it just the wind that came that night?
I knew not whence it came, or what it bore;
Was it, then, just wind, and nothing more?

2 / 2

"Tent *City*," it was called, I do declare,
And me the only occupant in sight!
Fought nameless demons, tossing turning there;
Somehow survived that first and frightful night.
I woke to sun, embraced the morning light.
Far down the road the sounds of life I heard.
Beyond, upon the hill, the radar site:
Technology's unchallenged final word.
So silent here, no dog, no bear, no bird
To calm the terror of my arctic dreams.
If arctic voice there was it went unheard;
Unheard in all the silence, so it seems.
I felt a million miles from all my friends;
Up here, the warming link to friendship ends.

The City

Prologue

Impenetrable silence generates …
What? Loss? For all the city's great estates?
Does this dismay, and occupy my mind?
"Joys" metropolitan I've left behind?
A mere moment's thought will soon refute
The city's grand untouchable repute.
Old Noah said it: "Cities aren't so hot.
Takes forty days to find a parking spot."

1 / 1

Despite the fear of solitude in tents,
That very solitude defined this place.
Around me: Snow; of garbage not a trace.
No city, this, where garbage gives offence.
In cities it's debris: The very word;
In cities: Always garbage centre-stage;
The Metro logo stamped on county's page.
In cities now *expansion's* always heard.
The beauty of surrounding fields means naught.
Indifferent fields there, waiting, dumb, like sheep;
The urban wolf will eat them while they sleep.
The wolf consumes the beauty, leaves a blot.
The beauty I recall? That used to be?
There, beauty's dead. Yes, beauty's fled, like me.

The Site

Prologue

A great idea, but like many, flawed:
A government by science fiction awed.
What else is new? When governments decide
On new (and costly) ways to stroke their pride,
The usual guys are there to foot the bill:
We keep the trough topped up, and always will.
And when, invariably, there comes the day
When all the costly toys become passé,
They're thrown away and new ones bought next week,
And U-know-who will turn the other cheek.

1 / 2

The Early Warning site's atop the Hill,
The radar site we're all up here to build.
With electronic mysteries it's filled;
A monument to our (and Yankee) skill:
A 30-metre ball, now empty, still.
For months constructors shovelled, dug, and drilled;
They see their efforts now almost fulfilled:
The bright, but mute, enigma on the Hill.
Few understand the reason why it's there;
– Or why *we're* there! – in all this barren ground.
This threat of enemy aircraft – *c'est la guerre!*
(A threat now empty as the land around.)
So much for sound and fury doctrinaire;
The huskies' laughter now the only sound.

2 / 2

At times around the early morning hours,
The dogs are all that's seen across the snow.
So occupied in their concerns, not ours,
Outlined against the site itself they go.
Just dogs and radar dome, with us below.
Above, aurora's shifting silken bands
Form patterns that expand, and spreading, glow;
The dog, though, neither cares nor understands.
I, too, know nothing, still I find it grand,
A land not grand – as "nice" – but grand in size:
Vast skies that soar above this boundless land,
Beyond the grasp of southern mind and eyes.
I try, but fail: I feel I'll never know
What wondrous gifts the arctic might bestow.

Paycheque

Prologue

Unending sky frowns down on louts like us.
With nothing else to do, we work, and thus
We work all day and sleep all night, and then
At sunrise, waking, do it all again.
For what? For money, that's the simple fact;
To get much more of what we've always lacked.
Intelligence will claim no place up here.
Take me: Full filled with smarts from ear to ear,
Yet, being clerical, I'm paid the least,
Fed crumbs, while dumbest of the dumb will feast.
I stand reminded: Life's like that, they say.
Stay dumb; intelligence is so passé.

1 / 1

Two hundred fifty dollars is my pay,
But then there's services, and room & board.
The charge? A dollar and a half per day,
Which leaves two hundred bucks as my reward.
Not much for this location unexplored.
It *was* my choice, and freely made, I know,
But still it's food for thought, and underscored
When snow storms are the first to say hello.
There's one more basic fact I've come to know:
A sign displayed upon the office wall
Explains it all in words so apropos;
A simple sign, quite short, yet says it all,
The blatant truth of which we're soon aware:
That "We're All Here Because We're Not All There."

Bunkhouse

Prologue

Up here is not a young man's Promised Land.
No Marilyn Monroe, no Sally Rand,
No sweet nocturnal limbs, no pretty face.
(A picture of the Queen will take their place.
Nice girl, but really not the stuff of dreams,
And rootless dreams are all we have, it seems).
Among our hundreds, most are still alone.
In bunkhouse built like doghouse, still alone.
Yet some will find a lively clique and swing!
With clicking spoons and stamping feet they'll sing!
Self-conscious celebrants, they'll sing awhile;
They'll push the night away and briefly smile.
But many, sunk in loneliness, and sad,
Remember friends and comforts that they had;
Reject the oh-so-basic bunkhouse state.
Yet, in their window, lonely pictures wait:
No image of the arctic's white and black,
Their face, alone, despairing, staring back.

1 / 2

The bunkhouse: built in minutes, it would seem.
The walls are boards; the doors fit, more or less.
The rooms are ten feet square, though at a guess
You'd call them *inches;* privacy's a dream.
The heat comes from an oil stove; fragrant steam
Now rises, all pervasive: socks, no less!
Atop the stove to dry with other dress,
That thus define our dwelling's spicy theme.
A central corridor runs east to west;
No ceiling, just the roof above your head;
Rooms left and right; the light? One bulb, at best.
For all the rest: the window near your bed,
That brings the North in wintery sunlight dressed,
To help us face the loneliness we dread.

2 / 2

Adverse conditions need a younger heart
To boldly face the fears to which you're prone,
Especially when you're here, a world apart
From all the southern comforts that you've known.
Unconsciously you feel: This, too, shall pass;
Discomfort's just another name for fun.
When golden dreams have subtly changed to brass,
You blithely think adventure's just begun.
If anything goes wrong, you're versatile,
A cool insouciant attitude will do.
You'll handle philosophically and smile
At all that Destiny will throw at you.
Indifference, or wit, is more your style.
You're smart. You know it all. You're 22.

Camp Manager

Prologue

When choosing managers, who did the choosing?
What oddball guides to choosing were they using?
Were choosers choosing losers? Did the chooser
Take the worst? To guarantee a loser?
It often seems the case when there's the need
Of managers for workers who can't read.
The ignorant can easily be swayed
By managers unschooled, un-MBA-ed.
The one we got could read and write, at least,
Though what he'd read seemed merely subleased
From sources somewhat vague and ill-informed,
Which then, by him, were pompously transformed,
Became his firm opinion, guiding light,
A light that frankly wasn't all that bright.

1 / 2

To burn the midnight oil was not his game;
Self-satisfaction served his ends quite well.
At Wisdom's door he stood, addressing Fame;
Awash in talent formed, to hear him tell.
And yet his every word would trust dispel:
Bizarre opinions aimed at pointless goals;
Opinions quick to change that would foretell
Days lost in thought of his divergent roles.
But we were generally pragmatic souls;
Decisions such as his we'd rarely heed.
We'd leave him there among his senseless goals:
Pagliaccio he, in every sense and deed.
He wondered why we never paid attention
To opinions of his very own invention!

2 / 2

Opinions formed by others shape our thought,
Inform our minds, lend depth to what was flat;
Some bring a welcome change to gaffes we've wrought,
Expand those views that frankly were old-hat.
But when bold Error sits where Truth once sat,
And fact's a stranger, though in fashion dressed,
Opinion should *in pace requiescat,*
To show us all that common sense is best.
But always there are those, with self obsessed,
Who say they've no opinion to confer,
Then quickly put its absence to the test,
And show in word and phrase how right they were.
Our manager had naught to say or teach,
And every day he'd prove it so in speech.

Lifelines

Prologue

It's one step forward, two steps back, in snow.
In brightly shining sun or twilight's glow,
Logistical appraisal of your route
From A to B, logistic-ly, is moot.
If, rarely, it's not snow, it's mud and muck,
The trucks in mire stall, the 'dozer's stuck.
And then the blizzard strikes: A two-day storm
Of horizontal snow on winds free-form.
The lifelines are the only highway then
To guide the cautious feet of sightless men.

1 / 1

Beyond my window, lifelines stretch, in sight
For maybe three short inches from my door,
And then they're lost within the snow's bright light;
Completely lost beneath the blizzard's roar.
I'm told by older hands just what they're for:
Step out the door—remember: *Don't let go!*
You're blinded by the snow; your eyes? No more
Will useful be; your hands alone will show
The way from A to B, as gasping, slow,
You cross the nightmare drifts: Insane terrain!
Your goal: Regain the next hut's fairy glow;
Through snow these lines your waning hope sustain.
O trembling thoroughfare! Hear hunger's call!
And lead me to the campsite's dining hall.

Food

Prologue

Up here, as in so many times and places,
There's men of many tastes and countless faces;
Of languages and practices arcane.
For unity of view you'll seek in vain;
Agreement is a stranger rarely met;
Political accord you'll never get.
Where's unity in such a polyglot?
Each day's full fraught with loud contesting thought.
I never felt agreement could be found
In this our Babel's cold infertile ground.
A single institution, though, unites us all:
Blind hunger's citadel: The dining hall!

1 / 3

So clear it is, and pure, the northern air
That works its magic on my appetite.
I eat all day — a moment's pause is rare —
Metabolism works both day and night.
I eat like a pig and never gain an ounce;
I'm tall and slim, with not a thought of weight.
I'll gain a pound and, horrified, announce:
"I'm getting fat!" (the guy you love to hate).
Another name for Heaven: Dining hall.
With twenty men per table: Noise and laughter;
Two steaks for lunch, potatoes, veg, and all,
And home-made bread, then pies, and cake thereafter.
Yes, full we'll be (with steak as appetizer!)
But (burp!) not necessarily the wiser.

2 / 3

The dining hall: a bunkhouse table-filled.
A score of trays of steaks, all yours to choose.
The service is straightforward, frills unfrilled,
Though wait. One frill: A knife and fork to use.
All this, of course, must heed the blizzard's voice.
Come storms, the steaks might change to canned
corned beef.
For three straight meals corned beef would be your
choice,
Till storm-bound planes returned and brought relief.
A stormy series, four days, maybe five,
Would make incoming planes our hunger's dream.
We'd lack supplies — like food! to stay alive
(And smuggled liquor, too, that some esteem).
We'd feel again the weight of arctic rages
That rampage over northern history's pages.

3 / 3

The campsite's food brings scores of memories,
Of years lost in the strip malls of the city.
Engaged, I was, in eating, more's the pity,
Along with all the fast-food devotees.
Eclectic strips of tiny enterprises
Where many hopeful businesses will strive,
Perhaps will win, with lots of luck and drive.
It's commerce rampant; many shapes and sizes.
The "restaurants" will serve the fat and thin,
The always-hungry ones who gravely seek
To gain the precious pounds they missed last week.
But sea gulls are the only ones to win:
"I've died and gone to Heaven," sea gulls smile,
And scoff the trash can's menu all the while.

Huskies

Prologue

To work or not: Can any of us choose?
For most it's work or starve – you win or lose.
For huskies, though, a lesson quickly learned
Was this: that ample food need not be earned.
Our camp provided gourmet treats galore:
The fragments of our steaks left by the door;
A bit of toothsome pie; a feast home-grown,
And never lift a paw – to starve's unknown.
And then to sleep the afternoons away,
A quiet belch, a snooze, no work, just play.
A belly full; no sleds to pull. No more!
Ignore the Inuit's voice, forget each chore.
No more those former days laborious;
No more the native boss censorious.

1 / 2

Deep night. The blizzard's stopped, though gusts still blow
Around the cookhouse, blowing, across the road,
And shake the power lines whose icy load
Now sways and glistens in the campsite's glow.
My bunkhouse window looks across the snow.
Along the cookhouse wall, where sand once showed,
Great drifts have swept the roof and overflowed,
And buried huskies sleeping there below.
They're lost to the living world, but undismayed;
Black nose within the snow the only sign
To mark the place where yesterday they played.
They'll wake to food, and females, too; they'll dine
On all that's left of steaks and pies homemade.
A husky's life; not bad, when I think of mine.

2 / 2

Our lives — the huskies' merry round, and mine —
In fact, bear little similarity.
For me, the work leaves nothing to define:
I'm occupied. If only by ennui.
But huskies are The Food Fraternity.
Though after this, like us, what's there to choose?
We're only similar to that degree;
Beyond a love of food — we work, they snooze.
Now we, to Great God Radar pay our dues,
While huskies eat, or sleep beneath the snow.
While one life bores, the other will amuse;
The doggies' dreams beat those *we* undergo.
The huskies chose free food; in this they're right.
But why did us guys choose this radar site?

The Song of the Wolf

Prologue

What wide wide world does separate us now;
How vain the words our alien tongues allow.
We touch – for one brief glowing moment seem
To understand … then eyes, so cold, agleam,
Tell more to me than any lips could say:
The interloper's me, in every way.
I came, but no one heard my trumpet call,
And when I go I'll not be missed at all.

1 / 3

The camp a resident white wolf supports.
Big girl, hip-high; of all the dogs she's boss.
The alpha male will shrug, accept his loss,
And then exchange his leadership for sports.
The males are not remiss by all reports;
The lucky huskies those who win the toss;
Pacific canine she, she comes across,
Provides the heirs; with every dog consorts.
She's pregnant now, and Harry (bunkhouse 3)
In agitation watches as she grows;
He's all the symptoms of a dad-to-be;
He's leaving soon — forever, I suppose —
But wants a pup, his very own, so he
Can take the North back with him when he goes.

2 / 3

Within the commissary window's glow,
Outside, just at the step before the store,
As patient as Time, she gazes at the door;
Once in, directly to the stove she'll go,
And brings indoors the tundra and the snow,
Adds mystery to the store's mundane décor;
Her mind seems placid, lost in lupine lore;
Grey eyes that understand what we can't know.
Then later, from my bunkhouse, I look around.
She's loping over snow … to where? And why?
Through pools of blackness on the treeless ground,
That vast extent of dark terrain and sky.
With that wild sky her untamed brow is crowned,
The Northern Lights agleam within her eye.

3 / 3

Her coat, once white, now stained by mud and sand,
So thick and coarse, once white as the snow around,
Once white as the snow in which she first was found;
Symbolic silence hers, just like the land.
Time pauses in her eyes. She seems to stand
As still and hard, unmoving, as the ground;
So still she is, just staring, not a sound,
Then moves away, ignores an outstretched hand.
Her days extend, without an end in sight;
No friend; Anticipation? None; no goal.
And yet, perhaps, far back in history's night,
Her canine memories define her role;
She looks within: another world, and bright;
Her northern heart, Aurora in her soul.

Puppy

Prologue

"A tragedy" might be too much, perhaps,
When many years, in time and change, elapse.
The subject, too, might slip beyond recall;
It's just a northern dog – a pup, that's all,
You'll see them, hundreds, everywhere you go,
And all up here, omnipresent as snow.

But tragic, yes, when all the hopes you've had
Are seen as empty as the land you're leaving;
The promises seen as deceiving;
A future now you can't believe in:
Empty Christmas stocking, friend. Too bad.

1 / 5

Big Harry is a warehouse man, and rough.
A great red-faced young ape, with attitude;
He laughs, and breaks the windows; Harry's tough:
He frowns, and bigger men will grow subdued.
But now the White Wolf's pups, much ballyhooed,
Are due, and Harry, just like us, can't wait.
For *us,* we'd simply like to see the brood,
But Harry is *involved* with sex and weight,
A single day's delay can't tolerate;
We hear no word but "dog" from Harry's mouth;
The *Second Coming* wouldn't be as great!
…'Cause Harry wants a pup to take down south.
Will girls cry "Wolf!" and fall beneath his spell?
The Master Of The North, and wolf as well!

2 / 5

The great day comes! Three pups, and one is male.
Big Harry plays the Dad to lupine son.
In conversation "doggy" words prevail;
Before Day 2 is done, his thoughts are one:
You greet him: "How are you?" The son-of-a-gun
Will simply smile: "The little guy is fine!"
Our Harry mightn't see another sun,
But never will the *puppy's* health decline.
And when we meet he puts his arm on mine
And lauds the paragon beside his cot,
Recalls each bark, consoles its every whine,
Recoils in fright: "The *fangs* the guy has got!"
He'll chuckle happily and then dash up
To gulp his lunch beside his fierce pup.

3 / 5

It's silver lining time for him and pup.
Big Harry's six-month contract soon will end,
And when those six long months are finally up
They'll fly down south at last, him and his friend.
But silver linings sometimes fade, and send
The grey clouds down to frown on us again.
One day the Mountie came: "I'm sorry, friend,
I hate to say, the pup's your loss, not gain.
The southern heat would drive the dog insane.
The puppy's habitat's the North," he said.
"When comes your time to leave, you'll board the plane
Alone." And our Big Harry hung his head.
To gambol down the painted days with pup;
To give his heart, give *all* … and then give up?

4 / 5

Since then Big Harry's joy has turned to pain;
Grey skies, that once by canine sun were blessed,
Are now just grey; the dog just Fortune's jest.
He moons around the pup, will watch in vain
Its bumbling passage'cross the floor's broad plain;
He'll kneel and crush the puppy to his breast.
Strong arms! It's hard to know who's more distressed.
Pup's pain will pass; Big Harry's pains remain.
The wolf/child whines, and tears blind Harry's eye,
His spirit lost, he's grieved beyond recall.
It wrenches heart and soul to see him cry:
Great hulking Harry, held by pup in thrall.
His face unshaven, grey, he still will try
To reassure the dog! The dog is all.

5 / 5

I think it shows how things are magnified
In isolation on this northern shore.
It's just a little animal, no more;
I mean, it's just a *dog,* all things aside …
Whose tiny paws held Harry's heart inside.
That dogs are sold in pet stores by the score
Did nothing for the sorrow Harry wore.
It seemed to us that Harry then just died.
But many years have passed. I wonder now —
Remembering Harry's laugh; the dog he had,
So briefly had, and sadly lost; and how
His every day was happy, never sad —
Did sadness pass then quickly from his brow?
Or stay, in sorrow's wretched garments clad?

Caterpillar

Prologue

The senseless arrogance of this machine
Is matched by all the drivers I have seen.
And both machine and man are built the same:
They're big, and hard, and loudly they'll proclaim
Their mastery, supremacy (how grand!)
And each, believe me, seeks the upper hand.
Each strives to show that he's the alpha male,
Will fight the other, straining to prevail.
Each day the mindless struggle is renewed;
And neither gives an inch, nor is subdued.

1 / 1

There's hardly any change between the two:
Machine or Man, when each to each is prey;
Mad partners in a violent ballet,
At odds, it seems, in everything they do.
Stout monoliths, the mighty Cats subdue
The Arctic soil, yet strive to disobey
Their master, Man, who also claims his say.
It's difficult to separate the two.
So often man seems more machine than Cat:
A second-class machine, and poorly made.
He knows the Cat's alive, and feels betrayed:
A new god sits where boastful Man once sat!
The proud machine by Man is undismayed;
It roars contempt, of Man is unafraid.

The Letter

Prologue

What joy when letters come from those we miss!
A happy word, a joke, a verbal kiss.
Each little thing that makes a life worthwhile;
Each loving thought, each word sincere, each smile.
But, ah! how tragic surely it must be,
When heartbreak waits for lonely addressee;
When letters come with news he longs to hear,
Yet offer not a word for eye or ear;
Where loving thoughts by him are never heard;
A distant unknown world in every word.

1 / 1

Light snowflakes drifting down on dunes of snow;
The window dark against the waning day;
The bunkhouse quiet now, the light is low.
The bulldozer driver's mind is far away.
With my soft words I keep the night at bay.
With "my" words? No, they're *her* words that I read,
And reading, will her loving thoughts convey,
And he each warm and wifely word will heed.
The Caterpillar driver cannot read,
And neither can he take up pen and write.
But I do both whenever there's the need;
An odd *ménage à trois,* you'd say. You're right.
It's I, strange medium, who binds their life:
Tomorrow I'm her spouse ... today his wife.

Old Pop

Prologue

You'd think you'd have an edge through education,
Your learning level seen in compensation.
You're wrong again, for dumb guys get paid well;
Among the highest paid of personnel.
There's some of us might like our framed degree,
And gain a sense of pride in PhD;
We studied hard and gained a wealth of learning,
But dumb guys win. They concentrate on earning.

1 / 2

Old Pop? Not scared of talk; recalls the past,
Old adages, and humour wise, homespun;
Philosophy; a rural pun rerun.
Short, 65, his best-before date's passed.
In youthful face and form by Youth outclassed,
Old Pop's a wrinkled unshaved son-of-a-gun.
He fills the bunkhouse oil stoves, sun to sun.
He's happy as a clam; his job will last.
But us? We come and go, like night and day.
André, the Frenchman, said that Pop's "Cray-zee!
He got no brain in head, dat's why he stay."
Oh yeah? Cray-zee like foxes, *mon ami.*
When so-called "crazy" Pop looks at his pay,
With *overtime,* it's *five* times more than me!

2 / 2

Up here, if you can count to two you're smart.
Old Pop just shrugs, with learning not obsessed.
With formal schooling Pop was never blessed,
And never sought what teachers could impart.
Each day you'd see him push his fuel oil cart
To bunkhouse, office, warehouse, and the rest.
At twenty-five below? Pop's not distressed.
His job's secure, he never will depart.
The storms? There's always one or more in store,
But Pop just laughs and slaps his knee with glee.
Can't read or write (not now, and not before),
But still, in irritation I can see:
Unschooled; not sure if 2 plus 2 is 4,
His paycheque's five times more than well-schooled me!

Money

Prologue

For scientists, and dentists, lawyers, too,
A single word, a gesture, each will do
To make them richer than their wildest dreams;
The less they do, the more they make, it seems,
Unlike the southerner up north, poor guy.
Well … maybe not so poor as I imply:
The money's here, and work will fill the day.
And every day there's overtime – more pay!
Just think: five times the pay down south's not bad!
And hey, no need to be a college grad,
No burning midnight oil, no tests to take,
No coeds, true, but still … no grades to make.
Up here there's some can't even read or write!
And if they could they'd not be here on-site.
They'd be down south, a two-bit job their aim,
And poorer be … for they could write their name.

1 / 1

Up here? No need to be a college grad;
No BSc; no framed degree.
Grade 4 is fine, if that is all you've had
(In fact, grade 4 would be a veritable PhD!)
Construction men, all kinds, all here, on-site:
Some tall, intelligent; some short and dumb;
I found that many couldn't read or write;
The Dumb outnumber Smart: Life's rule of thumb.
But smart or dumb, most sought the camp life's peace:
Uncomplicated, boring; lots of work, and sleep.
For recreation, "music" brought release
(Though combs and spoons might make the Muses weep)
But money brings them here, and brings them back:
Five times the bucks! and cannot write their *name!*
Yet, as they say, "All work, no play, makes jack,"
And lots of *that,* my friend; that's why they came.
They might not read or write, but what the hell?
To cash their cheques, an "X" works just as well.

Beer

Prologue

You'd think, with Prohibition, that we'd learn
That banning drink just makes the drinker yearn
For ever more of liquor's pleasures dubious,
Although they're not especially salubrious.
But notwithstanding banning, there were those
Who, quick to act when dry conditions rose,
Were there to slake our thirst (and grease their hand),
And prove the natural law: Supply, demand.

1 / 1

Construction sites are dry, or so they say.
Each day the so-called fact is proven true:
Great piles of empty beer cans block my view,
So, yes, we're dry—by *breakfast* every day.
Forget the breakfast, as the Mounties say:
"Whence comes this beer, and all this hard stuff, too?"
The answer, Mounties and constructors knew:
All turned, gazed south to where the Yankees stay.
Liquor, for the Yanks, was right at hand.
They had the right to drink, the American Way;
They had the only bar in this vast land;
The right to sell it, too, and boost their pay.
So thus the Mounties found, with contraband,
That every Yank "drank" forty cans a day.

Smoke

Prologue

There's Crime, and Punishment. Now, that sounds grim.
They're not the product of a passing whim.
Both crime and penalty are rarely nice,
And each in its own way will have its price.
And both can be unfair: The punishment,
Indeed, sometimes exceeds the law's intent,
And thus, itself, becomes a greater crime:
Some guy, all innocent, does serious time.
But some crimes never earn the title "grand."
They're barely misdemeanours, man. Take contraband:
The tax that would accrue from contraband
Would often in the tax man's pocket land.
So who cries "Crime!" when every eye is dry?
The tax man loses tax? Well, hey. Poor guy.

1 / 3

To smoke is detrimental to our health,
Though some will shrug and puff three packs a day.
They say well-being is a nation's wealth;
On site our wealth went up in smoke to stay.
We daily puffed four hundred packs, I'd say.
Was it, indeed, Canadian smoke? Oh no,
We saved a buck and smoked the Yankee way,
And aided them and us by doing so.
At thirty-seven cents our costs weren't low.
The Yanks could flog their fags for double cost,
To feed our shattered lungs and save us dough,
And we could tell our tax man to get lost.
The Yanks could stunt their growth for one thin dime,
And so could we, at twenty cents a time.

2 / 3

Our Yankee friends, shrewd chaps, did profits pluck
With both their hungry hands and larcenous ways
By selling us their ciggies by the truck.
Philosophers have said crime never pays.
They're right! Eventually there came the days
When *we* smoked US fags and Yanks had *none!*
Goodbye their inexpensive yesterdays!
It's thirty-seven cents for everyone!
The Mounties pondered how our store was run:
Buy low, sell high? A nice dishonest buck?
Was it the crookest game beneath the sun?
Was it in funds, the Yankees out of luck?
And so, with Yank's top brass, the Mounties came,
Checked books and stock, but found no one to blame.

3 / 3

The sellers by their own petard were hoist.
The Mounties and their Yankee peers conferred,
(Though Mounties smiled, ironic thoughts unvoiced),
And, quietly, decisions were deferred.
The planes — with cigarettes — again were heard;
Again we bought Yanks' ciggies, unsuppressed.
But in my mind an idle question stirred
That in that smokeless time went unaddressed.
"No comment," those wise Mounties said, if pressed.
But think: Would *honest* Yanks who bore the lack,
Who spent those days by cigarette unblessed,
Not seek a pound of flesh for every pack?
While Mounties and Yank brass condone they might,
O seller bold … don't walk alone at night.

The Plane

Prologue

The plane had crashed; so quiet now, so cold.
A toy-like fire engine still on hold
In case of further fires. Smoke lingers there.
Along the runway, previously bare,
The wreckage lies, propellers roughly bent,
The tail assembly twisted, engines spent.
What once flew like a bird before the crash
Is now inert, a smoking pile of trash.
I thought about the pilot, safe at last,
And what he felt, the terror finally past.
His brush with death so vivid in his mind,
Each precious second now so sharp, defined.
I wondered what he'd feel when next he flew.
Another plane … another landing, too.

1 / 2

We heard the crash, and ran outside to see.
It landed, bounced, then came down once again,
This time in flames, an engine falling free,
Propeller spinning gaily down the lane.
The fire truck comes speeding, siren wailing,
The firemen, hanging on like Keystone Kops,
Across the fields the siren slowly failing;
The flickering flame then gradually drops.
My thoughts were of the pilot's sudden fear,
The moment when the engine dropped in flame.
His life and limb, and all that he held dear …
Did he then see Death's face and hear his name?
I found him in his hut: Blind drunk, profane,
Recalling Death's hot presence in his plane.

2 / 2

Plane crashes aren't much fun, I've found,
Though funnier less if you happen to be on board.
Beyond immediate contact, though, it's sound
To think of long-term loss sometimes ignored.
A single storm, of two-three days perhaps,
Brings shortages of food and staff;
Machinery, too, will also feel the lapse,
And operating costs go off the graph.
These shortages just simply illustrate
The absolute importance of The Plane.
What happens when it's mail that we await?
Without the plane's long arm we'd wait in vain.
Up here a letter's valued more than gold:
A loved one's thoughts; a child's days told.

Fashion

Prologue

Construction sites are not with style obsessed.
No chance you'll suffer being overdressed.
No Ralph Lauren or Calvin Klein up here.
No need for them when drinking smuggled beer.
The acme of all style's Kenora mink:
A thick plaid shirt that takes its name, I think,
From logging camps and mines where it was worn:
Kenora, so they say, where it was born.
Kenora mink was thought by some to be
The northern fashionista's formal key:
Top button buttoned, man, to subtly imply
The boondocks' natty version of black tie.

1 / 1

Now fashion firmly frowns on golf's plus fours;
They once were *sine qua non,* but bless the day,
The garments now are golfing's dinosaurs;
Plus fours are gone and laughably passé.
But fashion calls us, too, in arctic climes.
The parka, here, is never out of style;
Kenora mink wears well in sunny times;
And — *de rigueur* — the heavy boot's worthwhile.
But now and then we'll think of southern days,
When heavy boots were rarely brought to mind;
When mink was what you wore to evening plays;
And when terrain to sandals was still kind.
But now we turn our back on old plus fours,
And dress accordingly for arctic chores.

Shirts

Prologue

The little things, in arctic isolation,
Assume proportions far beyond their station.
A shirt is just a shirt, all said and done,
And worn without a thought from sun to sun.
But shirts, if worshipped – glorified as art –
Well, sane restraint will flee, and sense depart;
When shirts are deified almost, and then
Subjected to the violence of men,
Our days are spent lamenting to excess.
Still, people have been murdered for much less.

1 / 5

His name was James. A lad of twenty-one,
From England came to us: Camp Polyglot.
Stepped off the plane, unique beneath our sun:
Well dressed! More fashion-wise than all us lot;
On fashion's A-list we were plainly not.
Despite the mud in camp his shoes were bright;
You knew his hat in Savile Row was bought;
His bag contained the only iron on-site.
His shoes were polished, pants were pressed each night.
The knife-like trouser crease would cut your hand.
Sincere; concerned that all he did was right;
Did all things well — while dressed so bloody *grand!*
How long, I thought, will he continue thus,
Till fashion's height is fashion's blight, like us.

2 / 5

The bath house, where — for those who're so inclined —
A morning wash can start your working day.
Some metal bowls beside four taps aligned,
And James: a well-cleaned bowl beside him lay,
With steaming water filled then borne away
To wash within his room, alone, unviewed.
Was solitude required to make his day?
To miss the morning crowd so loud and crude?
But there he went, with personal bowl accrued.
To thus avoid strange germs and bugs unknown?
To wash in peace, and prying eyes exclude?
Just simply shy, that he must wash alone?
Or does the Empire's heir, of course, refuse
To wash in bowls the common man does use.

3 / 5

About his shirts young James expressed concern;
Our laundry's rough-and-ready, short on frill,
And Fashion's trophy it will never earn,
Nor in our hearts a boundless faith instil.
His shirts, the product of the tailor's skill,
Were white, the finest cloth. "No starch!" he cried.
"No chance of that!" I laughed. James worried still.
Then, when the shirts came back … he almost died.
The shirts, the symbol of his British pride,
Were washed, all right; no starch … but they … were *pink!*
Sweet pink, dark rose, in patches side by side;
Good shirts, still sound, and hey, they didn't *shrink.*
James screamed his pain and anguish to the sky;
The only white shirts in the north — goodbyeee!

4 / 5

The laundry — all red flannel and red plaid;
It's shirts, and plaids, whatever: In she goes!
Poor James was wild; we laughed he was so mad.
To laugh is easy when they're not *your* clothes.
For James it wasn't easy, heaven knows,
The more he looked at those disgraceful shirts
The worse the shirts looked back, light pink, dark rose.
When nothing can be done, ah! that's what hurts.
He blamed the North for these unjust deserts;
No tailor's shop to clothing needs fulfill;
Shirt makers, none. Young James to plaid converts.
For weeks he muttered, wretched, furious still.
His words then bore a suffix, well-rehearsed:
"Food's bad ... *that laundry, though, must be the worst!*"

5 / 5

Those shirts would nevermore offend his back.
The camp's red plaid he donned against his will.
But none could ever say our James was slack.
Neck buttoned tight, and ironed fit to kill …
And yet: a subtle change. Well mannered still,
And clean; his fingernails immaculate;
Though much reduced, his clothes still showed his skill.
Industrious, efficient, neat … and yet …
Though all responsibilities he met,
The eagerness, desire to please, was gone.
But only Man a grudge will not forget;
Indifferent Time just shrugs, and passes on.
It won't be long before he'll curse and cuss,
And wear his plaid, be just as bad … as us.

Hudson's Bay Company Store

Prologue

Coureurs de bois – Radisson et al., and more –
Are thin on the ground around this frozen shore.
Alone along this icy sea we'll see
That leader of the world's explorers – me.
I'm dressed for everything but arctic climes,
And long for softer southern summertimes.
We'll see, that when the HBC post calls
Excitement quickly fades, attraction palls.
I'll find, quite frankly, if I had my druthers,
I'd rather leave the Hudson's Bay to others.

1 / 3

I'd heard the Hudson's Bay store was nearby,
A relic of the good old fur trade days.
I'd planned to go with Bill the warehouse guy.
I *thought* we'd drive, but "thinking" never pays.
Bill walked. So I walked, too, and duly froze.
I'd dressed to drive: in T-shirt there I stand.
No gloves. I walked, near nude, in summer clothes;
Five minutes: Lost all feeling in my hand.
Legs frozen; nose and fingers white as snow,
The endless drifts before, by ice held fast,
At last, we came, though how I'll never know.
The Hudson's Bay post! There! Our trials were past.
We came: The store snowbound, I found.
The post was closed. Of man no sight or sound.

2 / 3

From Heaven came proprietors: Two men,
In slippers, just to mock my frozen feet.
But once inside I thawed a bit, and then:
No beaver skins? No pemmican to eat?
And where was Nelson Eddy? Where was he?
And where his song of love and loss so sad?
Jeanette's brave singing cop, the stout Mount-ee,
Who saved her pulchritude from all things bad.
Nope, none of that; just all that's up-to-date:
Just razors, toothpaste, chewing gum and all,
And strangely these two men, marooned by fate:
Days gone, and those to come must surely pall.
I wondered at the life these two must know,
On this their social island in the snow.

3 / 3

The Hudson's Bay hegemony had waned.
The Hudson's Bay store: Home to them, those two,
But times had changed, though still perhaps retained
Some subtle flavour of the north, it's true,
But now the huskies bowed to Bombardier:
Machines! (The dogs will have to get a job).
And beaver skins are oh! so yesterday.
"But what else can we sell?" the store might sob.
And sob they will anew, and stock the store
With all the items *southerners* hold dear,
And basic salesman's skills they will ignore
While touting pointless piles of southern gear.
So, now the Bay will sell me chewing gum.
A giant step ahead, they'd say … for some.

Trust

Prologue

The banks don't trust. I, too, would rather not.
I've lost enough, and losing learned a lot.
Some natives, too, had been around the block,
And found that our "sincerity" was mainly talk.
They found that money played some funny games;
Our banknotes had odd colours, different names.
When red is two, but changes when it's blue,
Well, someone's bound to lose, and they knew who.
They now support the shrewd accountant's mind,
And all have been around the block, you'll find.

1 / 2

The natives here will barter any day,
But think a moment, friend: What would you do
With *banknotes* — different worth, and multi-hue;
With blues and browns of Canada, let's say,
Or all the same, from good ol' USA?
The native-born, arch-pragmatists, all knew,
With colours and strange numbers to construe,
There was but one sure way the game to play:
That each and every bill was held the same:
One bill, one buck; all else disdain;
"A two?" "Change for a five?" you'd say, in vain.
In early days their trust did mock its name.
But those born here learn fast, from trust abstain.
"One bill, one buck" is now their wise refrain.

2 / 2

And yet, why not this lack of open trust?
The past has seen them screwed by southern ways;
So-called "concern" indifference betrays;
Kind words when based on cash can be unjust.
They're little fellows, brown, bright-eyed with trust …
Well … once, perhaps, then found it never pays.
Now narrowed eyes each southern word appraise,
And like the Arctic wolf each act distrust.
But then the Commissary changed all that.
The native "shopped" and "cash" was never heard.
For him, some needles, thread; a nice plaid hat;
For us, the fur-lined glove that we preferred.
His purchases were billed to us, and that
Made film-flam's "trust" a much more friendly word.

Native Born

Prologue

We sometimes try to be what we are not.
Succeeding, then, we lose what good we've got,
And frequently retain the not-so-good,
Thus gaining nowhere near the good we could.
But worse, to seek what we are not, and fail!
When we, then, change our lives to no avail,
We forge an empty image, not our own.
In that sense we're unique: We're all alone.

1 / 3

He's native-born, and always tried to be
The man he'd never be: the Yankee's peer.
He'd worked with Yanks; the weather station's near,
A mile perhaps from him to the Land Of The Free.
He dressed the part: the baseball cap, big "B"
For Boston's team; Sox fan he was that year.
Dead cool: the mirrored shades, and all that gear;
The heavy flying boots … the Yank trainee:
The Stars and Stripes, mom's apple pie clichéd.
He strove to make "the boy next door" his role.
But "boy next door" was raised down south, homemade.
Why, even here he hasn't reached his goal;
He's still the native-born, in masquerade:
American … in all but heart and soul.

2 / 3

What function he performed I've never known;
He seemed just … there: I never heard his name,
Or where he ever went, or whence he came.
And when (and if) he spoke to you he'd shown
You were, in social caste, beneath his own.
He treated fellow natives just the same:
Aloof his attitude; contempt his aim.
And thus you'd often see him there … alone.
I wondered at the heavy price he paid
To be a Yank, and find success was slight.
To dress the part and play the role's charade,
Did he, believing what he did was right,
Now lie there in the thankless bed he'd made,
And thinking on it, lie awake at night?

3 / 3

I see him standing as before, and lonely,
Hands in pockets, mirrored shades agleam,
Haunting the periphery, and only
Posing in his cloak of self-esteem.
And his contempt apparently for me
— Everyone who wasn't Yank, that is —
Was matched by mine for him invariably,
Though left my soul quite tranquil, unlike his.
My life waits down south — from sea to sea! —
Circumscribed it's not by northern snow;
Bound by clime and culture his will be.
Yanks will leave, in time, but he'll not go.
To try to play the spurious Yank in vain
Will be his everlasting loss, not gain.

But Never Say Goodbye

Prologue

I'm drawn by northern mystery. Arriving,
Prepared to live here in the north, I'm striving
To make it home for one brief northern day.
Six months my contract says. Not much, I say.
My time has passed, and just as fast, up here;
I've got a lifetime, man, what's half a year?
My busy world down south? A memory.
For now a silent world is all I see,
A brooding, dark, immense expanse of … what?
A dense and soundless night; not what I sought.
I thought it would be just like home. It's not.
I've bought a silent world that time forgot.

1 / 2

Within the realm of taste our foreman fits.
No simple room would ever gratify.
A carpet's down, and chairs where comfort sits;
Soft music soothes, warm lamps will rest the eye.
The pilots of the Yankee base nearby
Are ready anytime for contraband.
Cigars? Cognac? They'll willingly comply,
And fly them in, despite the fact they're banned.
And so the foreman and a friend expand
In nightly talk of work, and love, and life;
Enjoy cigars, and chess, that's there at hand;
They welcome smoke and drink, and banish strife.
They've found, with pilots eagerly supplying,
A home-away-from-home that's satisfying.

2 / 2

"Eleven months," the foreman said. "Too long;
I can't support my solitary state.
My dreams and healthy sex just don't relate,
And real-time sodomy I *know* is wrong."
But soon he'll leave what he's enjoyed yearlong:
To sip cognac; on chess moves meditate;
Soft music, talk, discussion and debate,
Though knows his final days he can't prolong.
But he'll come back; he's said as much, and more;
To face the chessboard's challenge once again;
Enjoy a glass of cognac as before,
The music of the masters in his brain,
The music of the North beyond his door,
Aurora's *lumière* its great refrain.

Loneliness

Prologue

A distance of a thousand miles extends
From friends to here where friendly contact ends.
And everything ends here, I'd say. Each day
Strange hands now seem to push: "Go home," they say.
The early loneliness grows more profound;
All sense is flown, and aberration's crowned.

1 / 1

The southerners up North that I have seen
Are prey to more than loneliness; like me:
Bleak loneliness alone I could foresee.
The North is more; a place I'd never been;
A place, an elemental place, serene,
Yet alien, that certainly for me
Had then, has now, a lack, to such degree
I must go back, to southern clime, and green.
What troubles most is not to know wherefore;
To want to leave, but not know what or why.
What stirs me so beneath this Northern sky?
Relentless unseen hands will push me more,
Insistent hands that bid me southward fly,
And answer not a word when I ask why.

Leaving

Prologue

And still I feel the senselessness of leaving,
The recognition of my self-deceiving.
Though conscious of the wonders that surround;
Still loving, in a way, the sight and sound,
The beauty that's around me that I found.
And yet I go. The south and "home" still calls,
And heart and mind will breach the arctic walls.

1 / 1

Now comes the time I cannot understand.
While mercenary mind says *Stay,* I know
I'm right to heed my heart when it says *Go;*
And so I will depart this barren land.
My resignation's in, my bag's in hand.
My contract still has seven weeks or so.
Can't help but feel: So little time … why go?
To feel — just *feel* — not really understand.
Still blind I seem to arctic majesty;
Still deaf to northern siren song, and aye,
Ignoring still the spell of sea and sky.
And all the while my heart and mind agree:
The south still calls. I'll go, and not know why,
And feel the pain of that last word: Goodbye.

The Endless Sky

Prologue

What's left? A well-worn notebook's daily line;
A word or two inspired by thoughts benign.
A bunkhouse joke these lines sometimes invoke,
Like James' pink shirt; the cigarettes we smoke;
And Harry's pup, and natives' waning trust,
All gone now, all just part of memory's dust.
I like to think that memories abide,
But memories beneath Today will hide
And play the straight-man to the Present's bray:
"Today's the day; old Yesterday's passé."

1 / 1

It's still unknown, the North to me,
Still deaf to northern peace I am, and blind
To all its beauty that I left behind,
Exchanged for southern smog, polluted sea.
The peace, you'd think, would surely be
A magnet, for my memory designed,
But memory, with years, can be unkind.
It's still unknown, the North to me.
Yet, sometimes images will come to me:
A face … but no name rises in my mind;
Each portrait of the past remains unsigned.
Still there, but still unknown, the North to me.
Still there; though fading, plays its part,
Its magic murmur yet within my heart.

The Silence of the North

Prologue

I left. But thoughts about the north returned;
Concerned for fading memories, I yearned
At times, and seemed to, faintly then, recall
The Arctic's beauty, majesty, and all.
When others – those who'd never been, just dreamed
As I did, centuries ago it seemed –
When then they asked me: "What impressed you most?"
I'd pause, the images a clamouring host.

1 / 1

Magnificence of Arctic day and night;
The flight — the clouds! — of birds across the skies;
The skies! God! skies beyond my sight, so bright!
You'll see I'm right: you've but to lift your eyes,
As I did in the days when I was there.
You'll stare, so overcome, as I was then,
Of southerner's mentality stripped bare.
And there, ignored within Aurora's ken,
You'll stand, as we all ultimately do,
And sense anew that you … don't *matter* here;
That you and I appear, the foolish few,
Just passing through; come dawn we disappear.
When we with all our toys and noise are gone,
The North's unchanging silence will go on.

ABOUT THE AUTHOR

Alan D. Butcher was born in Vancouver, B.C. and has been writing all his life. He has written advertising materials, worked in the Canadian Arctic, and wrote and produced *The Chase Almanac* for 25 years. His published books include *I Remember Haida* (Lancelot Press, 1985), *Ale & Beer* (McClelland & Stewart, 1989), and *Unlikely Paradise: The Life of Francis Gage* (Dundurn Press, 2009). Alan has three additional books in progress: a novel, a memoir, and an urban social history book. He has won the 2010 Donald Grant Creighton Award for Best Biography from the Ontario Historical Society for his book *Unlikely Paradise: The Life of Francis Gage.* Alan lives in Cobourg, Ontario. He is a member of the Writers' Union of Canada.